In The Flow Of Life

The flow, where the life take unexpected turns.

Anisa Izar

Made with ❤ on the BookLeaf Publishing Platform
www.bookleafpub.in
www.bookleafpub.com

Dedication

Life has given us moments of stillness and change, shaping who we are. The relationships we cherished are valued, and new ones have emerged that are worthwhile.

Preface

This book explores the various moments in life that change our perspectives. Life is not always as it appears; it flows and transforms, often in unexpected ways. Even those whose lives seem perfect may be grappling with their own unseen struggles.

The book also shows the significance of relationships in our lives and how they shape our identity. It highlights the support we receive from both the bonds we formed early on and the new hope that arises from the connections we create later.

Self-realization is a crucial aspect of life. Even if we find only a few supportive figures in our lives, it is ultimately up to us to shape our experiences for better or worse. It's essential to understand that, in the end, it's you versus you. You are the only one who can address your problems, and you also have the power to make them worse.

This book illustrates that life presents both beautiful and heart-breaking moments. It is our responsibility to look beyond difficulties, even during the toughest times. While it won't be easy, we must confront challenges with courage to overcome adversity. Because at the end of the day, it's "YOU FOR YOURSELF".

Acknowledgements

I would like to begin by expressing my profound gratitude to my Creator, ALLAH, for bestowing upon me the incredible gift of expression. This divine quality allows me to articulate my thoughts and feelings, and to share the unique perspective I have of the world through the medium of poetry.

Next, I want to extend my heartfelt thanks to my wonderful parents, IZAR BUX and

MAIMOONA, who have always been my unwavering support system. Their encouragement and belief in me have been instrumental in helping me pursue everything I have ever aspired to achieve.

I cannot forget to mention my amazing sisters, *AYSHA SHAHID* and *SHAHISTA IZAR*. Their constant support and assistance in every conceivable way have played a crucial role in nurturing my writing journey.

Finally, I must express my sincere appreciation to BOOKLEAF PUBLISHING for providing me with this incredible opportunity to fulfil a cherished childhood dream of sharing my work with the world.

1. WHERE THE BEAUTY MEETS PEACE

Far from the busy and chaotic life,
Here lies the heavenly vacation site.

Where people from every state unite,
Living in harmony and delight.

We can see the history in every scene,

The lives of our ancestors cannot remain unseen.

Japanese bunkers, cellular jail, and many more,
My heart aches knowing their sacrifices from the time before.

You will see welcoming people with every step you take,
Unity here is something no one could ever break.

Andaman and Nicobar Islands, a place of love and peace,
Beautiful sites include beaches, waterfalls, and breathtaking coral

reefs.

Seeing its diversity, "Mini India"
we say,
Proud to say that, THIS IS THE
PLACE WHERE I STAY.

2. I HAVE SEEN IT ALL

I have seen it all.

Children running around me
with a cheerful laugh,
While their nanny spends time
with her better half.
The tears of the widow who has
lost the love of her life,
I have seen her here before with
him by her side.

I have seen it all.

*A girl posting flyers for her
missing cat,
The same one I saw last night
chasing a rat.
A couple teaching their little son
to ride a bike,
I remember seeing them here
when they were young alike.*

I have seen it all.

*But one day, everyone
disappeared from my sight,
And then someone placed a sign
that read "Construction Site."
Then I heard the loud noises of*

bulldozers and cranes,
It felt like a thunderstorm hitting,
without any rain.

I have seen it all.

The workers took shelter under
me when the sun was bright,
And continued to cut me down,
trying to finish before night.
Yes, I am dead now, but little do
they know,
I have contributed a lot for this
place to grow.

From spring to fall,
Yes, I HAVE SEEN IT ALL.

3. THE ART OF LETTING GO

My heart was broken; it needed repair,
But instead, it got hurt, scratch by scratch.

I thought he was holding my hand in despair,
But then I saw a knife in his other hand.

I ignored it because I loved him more,

And I didn't know the art of letting go.

He hurt me again, and then he smiled;
Seeing him, I realized this wasn't right.

I wanted to be free, but he wouldn't let me go,
Just because he didn't want to be alone.

All the promises he made were fake;
Not realizing it sooner was my mistake.

I let go of his hand and looked at his face,
I saw that realization, but it was too late.

Loving myself more was something I never tried,
But now, when I do, it feels all right.

4. THE BREEZE OF 2020

Freely wandering and observing the world,

Children are playing, and youngsters are in love.

Some people are happy, while others look sad;

There was a balance of emotions on this land.

But this year, nothing seems the same,

*As if the devil of sorrow has won
the game.
I can't see anyone outside their
house,
Only a few people, instead of the
crowd.*

*There is no laughter from the
children; no one appears happy,
Lovers are apart and feelings are
crappy.
Months have passed, yet nothing
has changed,
The fighters are fighting to free
us from this cage.*

*Many are depressed, staying all
alone,*
*Many people don't even have a
home.*
*What had happened to this
world?*
*Moments of happiness feel all but
garbled.*

*Is this any kind of curse on
human beings?*
*Or is the karma punishing them
for their deeds?*
*Abandoning parents, theft,
murder, rape and more,*

Day-to-day   crimes   leave
everything sore.

Good people will know the
nature's worth,
Bad ones will, every time, bring
out the worst.
Wake up, humans, there is still
time;
Try to be among the good ones,
and stop participating in crime.

Just a few small steps can make
the world a better place;
Your good deeds will rise, while
the bad ones can be erased.

*Wishing an end to this pandemic
from this land,
I long to see it happy and blissful
again.*

5. A VOICE WITHIN

Day by day, life goes on.

What have I achieved? What have I won?

I always tried to keep myself strong.

I dreamed big, but where did I go wrong?

I feel a lack of motivation,

A sense that I have lost.

I feel dead inside;

My soul needs a respawn.

*I want to be the best; I want to be
on top.*

*I want to fulfill all my dreams; I
just don't want to stop.*

*Who is going to help me next? I
wonder while I stand.*

*Then the voice within said, "It's
all in your hands."*

*I thought about what I did and all
that I ignored.*

*I should have faced my problems
in the time before.*

*It took me a while, but I finally
realized*

It's never too late to start;
I had just been holding myself
behind.

6. GENERATION GAP

Telling my mother that I am going shopping to buy new outfits and shoes,

To take some pictures and make reels to gain likes and views.

She said I could go, but this isn't how it should be;

You should rather dress up for yourself and be carefree.

Sitting at the table, I suggested,
Mom, let's order some food,
Like pizza, burgers, fries,
something that tastes good.
She nodded her head and said,
"This is not what you should eat;
We should rather cook some
veggies and prepare ourselves
some meat."

I then said, "Oh, Mother! I feel
like I am depressed,
It feels like anxiety is haunting
me, and I have a lot of stress."

She then replied, "There is
nothing like depression; it's all in
your mind,
Just stop using your phone so
often and always remember to be
kind."

I grew tired of asking why she
objected to everything I say,
Why she always had a different
opinion, I can't stay this way.
She then said, "My dear daughter,
I really don't know why,
I'm trying to do what's best for
you; come here, please don't

cry."

*She looked me in the eyes and
said, "My baby girl, it's all right,"
She wiped away my tears and
then hugged me tight.
Seeing her so concerned about
me, I finally realized,
That she is not wrong at all; we
just lead two different lives.*

7. THE RAINDROP REVIRE

Sitting on the balcony, I felt the cold breeze.
I closed my eyes and sighed in relief.

Then a drop of water fell from the sky;
It landed on the petal of a flower that was dry.

Suddenly, the rain started falling all over the place;
It felt like, for a while, all my worries were erased.

Outside the balustrade, I held out my palm;
Those cold droplets made me feel so calm.

The scene outside was something that couldn't be ignored;
Everything had become much brighter than before.

*I heard the birds singing as they
flew in the sky,
Finding shelter in trees to keep
themselves dry.*

*The harmony of the water
dancing in the pond,
Oh, the soothing effect of that
sound!*

*Rain comes as a blessing that
nature celebrates;
It brings hope, and the peace
regenerates.*

8. I FOUND MYSELF

There was a dream I had as a teen;
I wanted to be popular and to be seen.

To be perfect, to be the best of all,
Never worrying about challenges, never fearing the fall.

I loved gatherings and thrived in the crowds;

*Being a good girl to everyone
was what I thought about.*

*Sometimes I was a little naive,
but I tried my best;
I pushed myself beyond my
comfort to fit in with the rest.*

*Back then, I tried to be someone I
was not;
I never considered what I liked;
peace was something I never got.*

*Those days are behind me; now I
do what I please.*

*I focus on myself, and my
hobbies bring me ease.*

*I don't prefer crowds anymore;
solitude is what I need,
I surround myself with people I
love, the best ones indeed.*

*I've faced the challenges, and life
lessons were learned,
Now I am proud of everything
that I have earned.*

9. IF THE SUN AND MOON COULD TALK

Once the Sun and Moon had a talk,
Life on Earth was what they would unlock.
The Sun spoke of the day so bright,
While the Moon described the lovely night.

The Sun said, "I see the beautiful land,

With forests, deserts, beaches,
and sand.
You can see that too, I know,
But I see them in light when they
glow."

The Moon replied, "O Sun, you
are unaware,
Many find little joy in your
glare.
You don't know the beauty of the
sky in the night;
The world romanticizes having
my sight."

"I know the truth of the world,"
said the Sun.
"I see them live, I see them have
fun.
Yet all of them sleep when I am
gone,
Leaving you in the dark, all
alone."

"Do you think that's the case?"
the Moon did reply.
"The real truth unfolds under my
sky.
The true colours of souls come
out in the dark;

They cover them up, yet they leave a mark."

In the end of their conversation, they realized,
The world appeared different through each pair of eyes.
The Sun sees the bright and colourful day,
And the Moon reveals the beauty night displays.

10. ECHOES OF EMOTION

In a world filled with people, both good and bad,
There are far more emotions than just happy and sad.
It's impossible to feel only one emotion at a time;
Each feeling brings along a range of emotions in line.

A boy plays with his dog, filled with excitement and joy,

Amused as he watches his dog chase after a toy.
Meanwhile, a mother stands by, watching him play,
Concerned and worried, fearing he might stray.

A man kneels to propose with a ring in his hand,
His hand shakes with nervousness, love, and hope so grand.
As he asks, "Will you be mine?" her heart fills with delight,
She cried out of excitement, imagining their future, shining

ever so bright.

A woman leans against the wall,
her eyes brimming with despair,
Mourning the loss of her brother,
who is no longer there.
Loneliness envelops her; she feels
as if she's drowning in grief,
Believing she has lost everything,
she seeks solace or relief.

In every situation in life, multiple
emotions are shown,
Whether a person is surrounded
by others or all alone.

*Sometimes, emotions can become
overwhelming and grand,
Yet we must learn to remain calm
and withstand.*

11. THE FILTERED TRUTH

The light from the screen illuminates your face in the dark. The tap of fingers and the eyes spark.

You're surrounded by people yet talking to none; The addiction to social media has already begun.

Scroll, like, and repeat is just what you do.

*Do you genuinely think you
know the world around you?*

*The world isn't as perfect as your
feed shows.*
*Every story carries a secret that
no one knows.*

*You go to watch the sunset just
for a post,*
*Ignoring the people who matter
the most.*

*You share your smile but hide
your pain.*

Is this truly what you wish to gain?

Filters can't fix what's broken inside.
Seek what you desire where your heart resides.

You think there's ample time, but it slips away too fast.
Enjoy your youth while it lasts.

12. TIMELESS BONDS

In this stage of life, I remember few important roles,
The cousins I have are connected to my soul.
We are not siblings by birth, but we all bond so well,
I place my trust in them with all the secrets I tell.

Childhood memories of us playing hide-and-seek,

Each corner of grandma's house held a memory unique.
We played, ate, laughed, and cried together,
This bond will be cherished in my heart forever.

Sneaking into the kitchen at midnight, sharing an hour-long talk,
Every time we'd laugh, we ruined our plans for the morning walk.
We traded our emotions that no lips could dare,

Even the truths that were hard to share.

Being the laughter of my childhood and the comfort of my grown-up days,
How did you all manage to be perfect in so many ways?
Walking along the path of life, we grew up so fast,
But the echoes of our laughter still hold the past.

13. THE PURR OF HEALING

I sat and wonder how the world behaves,
Only to find more peace in my cats than in humans ever gave.
When I hug them, chaos turns to calm.
With them in my arms, life loses its harm.

I remember how, in my tough times, they stayed near.

With every purr, they gently calmed my fear.
They came to me and curled up by my side,
Bringing comfort that no spoken words could provide.

Even without language, their love is clear.
With them by my side, I never felt alone here.
Having their company feels too good to be true;
It's a special bond that only a few ever knew.

True love and affection are given
by my cats;
In return, all they need are some
gentle pats and food, perhaps.
When the world left me with
scars, they stayed with me,
And my life without them can
never truly be.

14. THE ONE WHO STAYED

I met you when my life was simple and the days were long.
You matched my vibe like the melody of a beautiful song.
At first, I thought we might not bond very well,
But now you have become the story I proudly tell.

We skipped classes and went to the park,

*Talking and laughing while
sitting beneath the trees' bark,
Sat for hours using the free Wi-
Fi,
As the waves danced under the
clear blue sky.*

*During tough times, I found you
by my side.
I share all my secrets that I
usually hide.
And when I cried my eyes out,
only in front of you,
You always turned my tears into
laughter, it's true.*

It's been years, and now no one could tear us apart.

You hold a very special place in my heart.

From college days to the chimes of wedding bells,

You stood by me through every season and all that life tells.

15. STILL HOLDING ON TO WHAT'S GONE

Some beautiful memories we made years ago.

It's still in my heart, I can't let it go.

You are the only one I needed by my side.

Letting you go gives me the pain I can't hide.

Nothing feels good, it's suffocating.

We are no longer together, those memories kept hitting.

That smile on your face, the way you looked at me.

It's all left in the past, our beautiful memories.

I used to love how you gently held my hand.

Those moments disappeared like water washing what's written on the sand.

I don't know where we went wrong

Because as far as I know our bond was very strong.

But now in despair I think about the time
When I was all yours and you were all mine.
We have lost each other is the truth we can't deny.
Time changed us, though we don't know why.

16. THE SELFLESS LOVE THAT RAISED ME

When life began, with the first cry,
Two gentle arms were standing by.
With eyes sparkling with love and joy,
In every glance, they find a child's alloy.

When growing up became hard to bear,

With their support, they were always there.
Through their care, they taught us to stand,
To thrive and bloom across the land.

I am nothing without both of you by my side;
Through all the tough times, I need you as my guide.
But when you're mad, I lose my ground;
Your silence is the hardest sound.

For all you have done, said, and shown,
With your love and affection, I have lived and grown.
Whatever I have achieved, and everything I do,
The start of my success began with you.

17. TIES BEYOND BLOOD

We met as strangers in this world so wide,
And somehow you chose to stay by my side.
I call you my older brother, and I mean it all;
You became my shield in every rise and fall.

In this world so fake, you are one of the few,

Having you as my brother is like
a dream come true.
You take care of me and give me
what I want,
Always had my back, never gave
a single taunt.

When I am hurt, you try to ease
my pain;
You kept your promise and stood
by me through loss and gain.
You boss me around like you're
twice my age,
And I listen to you like some
wise old sage.

You bonded with my family and became one of us;
Now even my parents love you without any fuss.
There is no blood connection; we don't share a family tree,
Yet you've become an older brother to me.

18. GROWING TOGETHER

Let me tell you about the one I hold dear,
Through every week and year,
we stayed far yet near.

She is my only sibling, and I cherish her so;
The one who knows all my versions, year after year, as we grow.

She's the only one who drives me
crazy yet brings me delight,
She's my perfect other half in
every situation, my guiding
light.

We argue like the world is about
to fall apart,
But even though she holds a
special place in my heart.

Whenever I become a mess, she's
right by my side,
Though she's younger, I adore
how in her wisdom I can
confide.

We face countless challenges, but together we stand strong,
With every step taken with her, I know I truly belong

19. UNWRITTEN CHAPTERS

We sit and wonder about the days gone so fast,
Planned a lot to do, but they never seem to last.
We drown in regret, losing all the hope,
Think that there is nothing left with strength to cope.

Between the hardship and regret, we forget,

That this is not the end; we have a lot more to get.
It can either be what you want, but it can also be worse,
You should know that it's just the process; it will surely be reversed.

Many lose hope in between and never find the light,
Some even end their lives, thinking that's what's right.
But little did they know there was hope waiting in the way,
Giving up so fast makes all the good things go away.

Some chapters have not been written in life yet,
Your hard work and struggle decide what you're going to get.
In every dark hour, in every storm we face,
We have to hold on to something, a light in our embrace.

20. THE MEANING THAT LOST IN THE NOISE

I usually prefer to be silent and calm,
I want to live a life without causing any harm.
But sometimes it's difficult to explain what I mean,
Because whatever I say often goes unseen.

I spoke calmly, but they heard what their heart wants,

I used simple words, and all they heard was taunts.

In their noise, I lost my own tone,

Until I learned to hold my truth all alone.

They even drew meaning from my sigh,

Listening to them shout, I hopelessly stand by.

I grew tired and gave up on what I wanted to say,

Because I realized they were going to stay this way.

*Finally, I understood that if they
didn't want to understand.
I wouldn't just sit here, offering
my hand.
Now I don't beg to be defined;
I smiled, ignored them, and freed
my mind.*

21. FAR FROM HOME

When I was young, still studying in school,

Living at home never quite felt cool.

I dreamt of cities with lights that gleam,

And moving out became my golden dream.

When college came, I seized the chance,

With hopes packed tight and a distant glance.

My suitcase full, my heart in flight,

Chasing freedom, chasing light.

I longed to grow, to stand alone,

To build a world that was my own.

But soon I found, beneath the thrill,

A quiet ache I couldn't fill.

Nervously I walked through the college ground,

Lost in a maze of unfamiliar sound.

No familiar laughter, no known face,

Just empty echoes and a crowded space.

And when finally it was night, the time to sleep,

Missing my home, I quietly weep.

The creak of home, my cozy bed,

The gentle touch upon my head.

I longed again for mom's embrace,

The smell of food, of my place.
I forgot the dreams I once had
packed,
Just wanted my old life back.

But slowly, in that silent fight,
I found my strength, I found my
light.
For even though I felt alone,
I learned to carry pieces of home.